Paul Gayler is executive chef at The Lanesborough in London, one of the most fabulous destination hotels in the world. He has worked in some of London's most prestigious restaurants, including The Dorchester and Inigo Jones. Paul has appeared on BBC2's *Saturday Kitchen* and Radio 4's *VegTalk*, as well as being a judge on ITV's *Chef of the Year*. His previous books for Kyle Cathie have been translated into 10 languages and sold 500,000 copies worldwide.

Paul Gayler's **little book of**
soups

Paul Gayler's little book of

soups

appetising, warming, brimming with flavour

Kyle Cathie Limited

For the New Age foodies who demand quality, taste and innovation.

First published in Great Britain in 2009 by
Kyle Cathie Limited
122 Arlington Road
London NW1 7HP
www.kylecathie.com

ISBN 978 1 85626 841 7

Text © 2009 Paul Gayler

Edited by Barbara Bonser
Designed by Mark Jonathan Latter @ Pink Stripe Design
New photography by Will Heap
Styling for new photography by Sheiko and Silvana Franco
Other photographs by Gus Filgate, Steve Baxter, Lisa Linder, Steve Lee and Georgia Glynn Smith

Paul Gayler is hereby identified as the author of this work in accordance with Section 77 of the Copyright, Designs and Patents Act 1988.

A Cataloguing in Publication record for this title is available from the British Library.

contents

introduction

Soups can be light enough to be served as starters or hearty enough to satisfy as main meals. The two basic components are a good stock and flavourful raw ingredients. Soups fall into two broad categories, clear soups and thick soups.

clear soups

Clear soups or consommés should be crystal clear, full of flavour and a lovely colour ranging from light gold to amber. They are time-consuming to make, since the stock is clarified through a layer of egg white. Consommés can be hot, cold or even iced in some cases. Broths are the simplest form of soup, stocks with meat, poultry or game added along with vegetables and other garnishes such as pasta. Bouillion is a clear stock minus the clarification process.

thickened soups

These are classified by the type of thickening agent used. Pureés are vegetable soups thickened with starch. Cream soups are generally purée soups finished with cream. Other ingredients used to thicken soups and broths include rice, tapioca, semolina, breadcrumbs or crushed nuts as well as different types of flour and grains.

chowders

These soups are traditionally made with fish, shellfish and vegetables, all left floating in the soup when served.

bisques

These puréed shellfish soups are highly seasoned with Cayenne pepper, flavoured with brandy, and thickened with cream.

fruit soups

These are generally served cold but can be served warm. Hot fruit soups appear in Middle Eastern and Chinese cuisines.

Asian soups

These typically broth-style soups are flavoured with Asian ingredients and aromatics such as soy sauce, fish sauce and tofu.

soup tips

• All soups can be stored in the fridge for 3–4 days, those made with fish or shellfish for 1–2 days only.
• You can freeze most soups and home-made stocks for up to 4–6 months.
• Do not add cream to a soup you intend to freeze, but add it once it is defrosted, when you reheat and plan to serve it.
• All recipes serve 4 people.

vegetable stock

2 tablespoons olive oil
1 onion, chopped
1 small leek, chopped
75g celeriac, chopped
2 large carrots, chopped
1 celery stick, chopped
75g white cabbage, chopped
½ head fennel, chopped
4 garlic cloves, chopped
125ml white wine (optional)
4 black peppercorns
1 sprig fresh thyme
1 bay leaf
1.5 litres water
2 teaspoons salt

Heat the oil in a large saucepan, add
all the vegetables and the garlic and
cook gently for about 5 minutes until
softened. Add the wine, if using, then the
peppercorns, thyme, bay leaf and water.

Bring to the boil, add the salt and simmer
for 40 minutes, until reduced by a third of
its original volume. Strain through a fine
sieve and leave to cool.

chicken stock

2.kg raw chicken carcasses, or chicken wings
    and legs
350g onions, chopped
350g carrots, chopped
150g celery, chopped
1 leek, chopped
1 bouquet garni

Put the chicken in a large saucepan, cover
with cold water and bring slowly to the
boil. Skim off any impurities that rise to
the surface, then add the vegetables and
bouquet garni. Simmer very gently for
4 hours, then strain through a fine sieve
and leave to cool.

meat stock

90ml vegetable oil
900g beef or veal bones, chopped into
    small pieces
450g beef or veal trimmings
3 carrots, chopped
2 onions, chopped
1 celery stick, chopped
2 garlic cloves, crushed
50g tomato purée
1 bouquet garni

Preheat the oven to 220°C/425°F/gas mark 7.
Heat half the oil in a roasting tin, add the
bones and roast for 30 minutes. Meanwhile,
heat the remaining oil in a large pan and fry
the meat trimmings until well browned.

Add the bones, vegetables and garlic to
the pan, cover with water and bring to
the boil. Skim off any impurities, then
stir in the tomato purée and bouquet
garni. Simmer over a low heat for 2 hours,
skimming frequently. Strain through
a fine sieve and leave to cool.

hearty winter soups

This well-made soup is both inexpensive and satisfying, and can be served as a starter, a light meal or a main dish. It is easy to prepare and forms the base for many different variations. Served chilled, it becomes the classic vichyssoise.

potato & leek soup

potage parmentier

25g unsalted butter
½ onion, sliced
2 large leeks, white part only, sliced
1 litre chicken stock
350g floury potatoes, peeled and
    chopped
120ml double cream
1 tablespoon chopped chives
salt and freshly ground black pepper

Heat the butter in a pan, add the onion and leeks, then cover and sweat until tender but not coloured. Pour in the stock and bring to the boil. Add the potatoes and simmer for 25–30 minutes, until they are tender.

Pour the soup into a blender and blitz to a very smooth purée. Return to the pan, reheat gently and stir in the cream and some seasoning. Serve immediately, sprinkled with the chives.

PG TIPS
Here are some of my favourite variations of this basic soup recipe. Add fresh herbs – stir in 75g finely chopped tarragon, chervil or parsley with the cream and serve chilled. For hot soup variations, add 200g blanched baby spinach with the onion and leeks, or replace the leeks with celery.

andalusian fish soup

with crusty bread

100ml olive oil
1 onion, finely chopped
2 garlic cloves, crushed
½ teaspoon dried chilli flakes
1 small bay leaf
½ teaspoon ground cumin
1 teaspoon grated orange zest
a good pinch of saffron strands
1 litre fish stock
300g mixed shellfish
  (such as mussels and clams)
3 slices of white bread
1 teaspoon tomato purée
1 teaspoon smoked paprika
450g mixed fish fillets
  (such as monkfish, snapper
  and cod), cut into 2.5cm pieces
salt and freshly ground black
  pepper

for the aïoli
1 garlic clove, chopped
a good pinch of saffron strands
1 tablespoon lemon juice
150ml good quality mayonnaise

Heat half the oil in a large pan, add the onion and cook for about 8 minutes, until tender. Add the garlic, chilli flakes, bay leaf, cumin, orange zest and saffron. Pour in the fish stock, bring to the boil and simmer for 10–15 minutes.

Meanwhile, clean the mussels and clams under cold running water and pull out the beards from the mussels. Discard any open mussels or clams that don't close when tapped on the work surface.

Soak the bread in a little water, squeeze it dry, then place in a blender with the tomato purée, smoked paprika and the remaining oil. Process to a paste and add to the soup. Carefully add the fish to the soup and simmer gently for 5 minutes. Add the shellfish and cook for 3–4 minutes, until the shells open. Season to taste and keep warm.

To make the aïoli, crush the garlic and saffron in a mortar with the lemon juice and then stir into the mayonnaise.

Divide the fish and shellfish between 4 serving bowls and pour over the broth. Serve with the aïoli, plus some good crusty bread to mop up the juices.

Nettles grow almost everywhere, so why not use them in this nourishing soup?

potato, smoked bacon & nettle soup

75g unsalted butter
1 onion, diced
1 leek, thinly sliced
600g waxy potatoes, peeled
    and cut into 1cm cubes
750ml chicken stock
100g nettles
300ml single cream
freshly grated nutmeg
salt and freshly ground black
    pepper
75g smoked bacon, cut into
    small dice
2 slices of white bread, crusts
    removed, cut into 1cm dice

Heat 50g of the butter in a heavy based pan, add the onion and leek and sweat for 8–10 minutes, until soft. Add the potatoes and cook for 5 minutes. Pour in the stock and bring to the boil, then reduce the heat and simmer for 25–30 minutes. Meanwhile, blanch the nettles in a large pan of boiling water, drain well and squeeze out the excess water.

Remove half the soup from the pan and blitz to a purée in a blender. Pour it into a clean pan, add the cream, nettles, the remaining soup, grated nutmeg and some seasoning and bring to the boil.

Meanwhile, heat the remaining butter in a pan, add the bacon and diced bread and cook until golden. Pour the soup into 4 bowls, sprinkle over the bacon and croûtons and serve.

PG TIPS

Pick the nettle tops in spring, when they are young and tender, and wear rubber gloves! Wash well before use and don't worry – once cooked, they lose their sting.

butternut squash & cannellini bean soup

150g dried cannellini beans, soaked
   overnight and then drained
4 tablespoons vegetable oil
1 onion, chopped
1 clove garlic, finely chopped
1 celery stick, chopped
½ teaspoon ground cumin
1 large butternut squash, peeled and
   cut into 1cm dice
5 tablespoons tomato passata
   (see page 97)
1 tablespoon chopped rosemary
salt and freshly ground black pepper

Put the cannellini beans into a saucepan, cover with water and bring to the boil. Reduce the heat and simmer for 1½ hours or until tender, then drain. Reserve the cooking water.

Heat the oil in a large saucepan, add the onion, garlic, celery and cumin and cook for about 5 minutes until the vegetables are tender. Add the diced butternut squash and mix in well. Pour in the reserved cooking liquid from the beans, bring to the boil, then reduce the heat and cook gently for 10–15 minutes, until the squash is soft and tender. Remove half the cooked squash from the pan and set aside. Add the tomato passata and cook for a further 10 minutes.

Pour the soup into a food processor and blitz to a smooth purée, then pour it into a clean pan. Bring it back to the boil and add the rosemary, cooked cannellini beans and reserved butternut squash. Heat through, then season to taste and serve.

I actually created this soup by accident when, after a recent Halloween party for my youngest child, I came across an uncarved pumpkin. The smoked paprika gives it a warming flavour – just the job for a winter's day!

smoked pumpkin & tortilla soup

1½ tablespoons olive oil
600g pumpkin, skin and seeds removed, cut into small pieces
½ tablespoon smoked paprika
1 onion, chopped
1 leek, white part only, chopped
2 garlic cloves, crushed
4 corn tortillas, broken into small pieces
850ml chicken or vegetable stock
100ml skimmed milk
2 tablespoons chopped flat leaf parsley
freshly ground black pepper

Heat the olive oil in a non-stick pan. Dust the pumpkin pieces with the smoked paprika and fry in the pan with 2 tablespoons water, covered with a lid, to colour them lightly. This should take about 10–12 minutes.

Add the onion, leek, garlic and tortillas, replace the lid and sweat the vegetables for a further 8–10 minutes.

Pour in the stock and bring to the boil, then reduce the heat to a simmer and cook for 20 minutes until the pumpkin is soft. Add the milk and stir well. Pour into a blender and blitz to a smooth purée, then return to the pan to reheat.

Add the parsley, season with black pepper to taste and serve.

Cullen skink can vary from a broth to a thickened soup, as in this recipe. When I think of smoked haddock I always think of soft poached eggs as an accompaniment, so I decided to add them to this traditional Scottish soup and discovered a real winner.

cullen skink

smoked haddock & potato soup

450g natural smoked haddock, on the bone
600ml hot full fat milk
2 onions, sliced
1 blade of mace
600ml water
75g unsalted butter
4 medium sized floury potatoes, peeled and diced
freshly grated nutmeg
salt and freshly ground black pepper
4 tablespoons vinegar
4 eggs
2 tablespoons chopped parsley

Put the smoked haddock in a saucepan, pour over the hot milk and add half the onion and the mace. Bring just to the boil, then add the water. Bring back to the boil and simmer for 4–5 minutes, until the fish is cooked. Remove from the heat, take out the fish with a slotted spoon and place in a bowl to cool. Strain the cooking liquid and set aside. Flake the fish, removing the skin and bones.

Melt the butter in a large pan, add the remaining onion and cook until soft. Add the potatoes and sweat for 5 minutes. Pour over the reserved cooking liquid and simmer until the potatoes are tender. Pour into a blender and blitz to a purée, then pour into a clean pan. Season with nutmeg, salt and pepper, stir in the flaked fish and keep warm.

To poach the eggs, bring a litre of water to the boil, add vinegar and reduce to a simmer. Crack in the eggs and cook gently for 2–3 minutes, then remove from the pan and drain well. Pour the soup into 4 soup bowls, place a poached egg in the centre of each portion and sprinkle over the parsley.

cauliflower
& olive soup

1 medium cauliflower, cut into
  florets
3 tablespoons virgin olive oil
10g unsalted butter
1 onion, chopped
1 small leek, white part only,
  chopped
750ml chicken or vegetable stock
150ml full-fat milk
85ml double cream
6 black olives, stoned, rinsed,
  dried and very finely chopped
salt and freshly ground black
  pepper
1 tablespoon chopped chives

Blanch the cauliflower florets in a pan of boiling salted water
for 2 minutes, then drain well.

In a large pan, heat 1 tablespoon of the oil with the butter,
add the onion and leek and sweat until tender. Pour in the
stock and milk and bring to the boil. Add the cauliflower,
then reduce the heat and simmer for 15–20 minutes, until
the cauliflower is almost puréed. Place in a blender or food
processor and blitz until smooth. Return to the pan, add
the double cream and olives and lightly season to taste
– remember the olives are already salty.

To serve, pour into soup bowls, drizzle over the remaining
olive oil and sprinkle over the chives.

PG TIPS
Whenever using olives in a recipe, I find it best to add them
at the end of the cooking. This helps them retain their shape
and texture, but more importantly prevents their salty
flavour from overpowering the dish.

Here a rustic soup made from the humble potato is transformed into something magical with the addition of creamy goat's cheese, lifted with a little truffle oil.

potato & goat's cheese soup

50g unsalted butter
1 onion, chopped
200g leeks, sliced
200g potatoes, peeled and diced
900ml chicken stock
100ml double cream
75g goat's cheese
1 tablespoon white truffle oil
salt and freshly ground black pepper

Heat the butter in a large pan, add the onion and leeks and cook over a low heat for 8–10 minutes without colouring. Add the potatoes and cook for a further 3 minutes. Add the stock and bring to the boil, then reduce the heat and cook for 15 minutes.

In a separate pan heat the cream to the boil, then stir in the goat's cheese and allow it to melt.

Place the potato soup in a blender and blitz to a purée. Mix in the goat's cheese cream and the truffle oil. Season to taste and serve immediately.

PG TIPS
Jerusalem artichoke and cauliflower are equally successful alternatives to potato. The soup should be the consistency of single cream. If it is too thick, simply thin down with more chicken stock.

In Britain, modern cooks are rediscovering the full flavour of whole grains like spelt. They have long been popular in Europe, especially Italy, where spelt is known as *farro* and is used in all manner of tasty dishes. It is very nutritious and the perfect answer for those people who want to eat good, hearty grain products. Spelt is available from health food shops.

spelt soup

with Jerusalem artichokes & saffron

150g fine spelt (preferably
  organic)
50g unsalted butter
1 onion, chopped
1 garlic clove, crushed
300g Jerusalem artichokes, well
  scrubbed and thinly sliced
6 fresh sage leaves
pinch of saffron
750ml good vegetable stock, hot
150ml single cream
salt and freshly cracked black
  pepper
40g pecorino cheese
1 tablespoon extra virgin olive oil

Soak the spelt overnight in a bowl of cold water and drain.

Melt the butter in a pan, add the onion and garlic and cook for 3–4 minutes until slightly softened. Add the artichokes, sage and saffron and mix well. Pour in the hot vegetable stock and bring to the boil. Add the spelt, cover and simmer gently for 20–25 minutes or until the artichokes are tender.

Reserve about 4 tablespoons of the cooked spelt for the garnish. Transfer the remainder to a food processor and blend until smooth, then return the soup to a clean pan. Add the cream and return to the boil. Season with salt and freshly cracked black pepper.

Meanwhile, grate the pecorino cheese as finely as possible and mix it with the reserved spelt in a bowl. Divide the soup between 4 serving bowls, sprinkle over the spelt and pecorino mixture and drizzle over the olive oil. Serve immediately.

chickpea & lentil mulligatawny

with spicy yogurt

25g unsalted butter
1 onion, finely chopped
1 garlic clove, crushed
1 teaspoon dried red chilli flakes
¼ teaspoon ground turmeric
125g chickpeas, soaked in water
  overnight and then drained
2 tablespoons prepared curry paste
1 tablespoon gram (chickpea) flour
1 litre chicken or vegetable stock
125g Puy lentils
1 tablespoon mango chutney
1 Granny Smith apple, peeled, cored
  and chopped
400ml can coconut milk
salt and freshly ground black pepper
2 cooked smoked chicken breasts,
  skin removed and meat shredded

for the cumin yogurt
½ teaspoon cumin seeds
6 tablespoons Greek yogurt

Melt the butter in a pan, add the onion, garlic, chilli flakes and turmeric and cook over a low heat until softened. Add the soaked chickpeas and curry paste and cook for 5 minutes, then sprinkle over the gram flour and stir it in. Pour on the stock and bring to the boil, then simmer for 2 hours topping up with more liquid if it begins to get too dry. Stir in the lentils and simmer for 30–40 minutes, then add the mango chutney and apple and cook for another 20 minutes.

For the cumin yogurt, toast the cumin seeds in a frying pan over a low heat until they are slightly darker and release their fragrance. Transfer to a spice mill or pestle and mortar and grind to a powder. Stir the cumin into the yogurt and set aside.

Pour the soup into a blender and blitz to a smooth purée. Return to a clean pan, add the coconut milk and bring to the boil. Season to taste and serve, topped with the shredded smoked chicken and a little cumin yogurt.

This hearty soup, originating from Puerto Rico, is ideal for a one-pot meal. Traditionally the soup contains a long list of ingredients, including rice, but everybody has their own combination, handed down over the years. Serve with lots of chunky bread.

asopao

(chicken paella soup)

1 tablespoon unsaturated oil
1 large chicken breast, skinned and cut into fine strips
1 small onion, finely chopped
2 garlic cloves, crushed
1 teaspoon chopped oregano (or pinch of dried)
¼ teaspoon dried chilli flakes
200g tinned chopped tomatoes
75g long-grain rice
1 red pepper, deseeded and chopped
50g cooked lean ham, chopped
700ml chicken stock
1 tablespoon green olives, pitted and chopped
1 teaspoon superfine capers, rinsed and drained
50g cooked green peas
freshly ground black pepper

Heat the oil in a non-stick pan, add the chicken strips and fry over a high heat until golden. Lower the heat, add the onion, garlic, oregano and chilli flakes and cook for 2–3 minutes.

Add the tomatoes, rice, red pepper and ham. Pour over the stock, bring to the boil, lower the heat and simmer for 25–30 minutes.

Finally, add the olives, capers and peas, adjust the seasoning with black pepper and serve.

PG TIPS

This soup is packed full of flavour and goodness, but it also takes a little time to prepare. The beauty of this soup is that it can be made the day before and reheated gently when needed.

This variation on the classic French onion soup replaces the usual white wine and Gruyère with ingredients from Normandy – beer and Camembert cheese. I have successfully replaced the Camembert with Carré de l'Est, which is milder in flavour and has a delicate aroma when ripe. You can, of course, use grated Gruyère or Emmenthal for a more traditional onion soup.

French onion soup

with beer & camembert

75g unsalted butter
300g onions, finely sliced
½ tablespoon sugar
1 tablespoon plain flour
1 teaspoon tomato purée
100ml light beer
1 litre meat stock
1 ficelle (small, thin baguette) or
  2 crusty bread rolls, thinly sliced
  and toasted
100g Camembert, rind removed,
  thinly sliced
salt and freshly ground black pepper

Heat the butter in a heavy based pan, add the onions and sugar and cook over a medium heat for at least 20 minutes, until very soft, golden and caramelised. Stir in the flour and tomato purée and cook for 2 minutes, until they brown very slightly. Pour in the beer, bring to the boil and after 1 minute add the stock. Reduce the heat and simmer for 15–20 minutes, then season to taste.

Pour the soup into 4 heatproof soup bowls or 1 large tureen and float the toasted bread on top in a single layer. Cover this with the Camembert slices. Put the bowls under a hot grill (or in a hot oven) until the cheese forms a well-browned crust. Serve immediately.

Puy lentils are the best lentils for this earthy rustic-style soup.
Not only do they taste wonderful, they also hold their shape
well during cooking.

puy lentil bouillabaisse

with spinach, fennel & saffron

for the rouille
1 medium-sized potato
1 small garlic clove, crushed
1 small red pepper, roasted and
  peeled
1 free-range egg yolk
pinch of good quality saffron (or
  powdered)
salt, freshly ground black pepper and
  pinch of Cayenne pepper
3 tablespoons extra virgin olive oil

2 tablespoons olive oil
1 onion, chopped
2 garlic cloves, crushed
pinch of good-quality saffron (or
  ½ teaspoon powdered saffron)
1 small head of fennel, cut into
  ½ cm dice
½ teaspoon fennel seeds
175g Puy lentils
½ teaspoon mild paprika
1 litre good vegetable stock
100g baby spinach leaves
4 slices of country-style bread, cut
  into 1cm cubes

For the rouille, cook the potato in its skin in a pan
of boiling water, remove and, when cool enough to
handle, peel off the skin. Place the garlic and pepper
in a blender and blitz to a purée. Add the cooked
potato, egg yolk, saffron, salt, pepper and a good pinch
of Cayenne pepper. With the motor running, gently
pour in a thin stream of oil through the funnel at the
top, until it thickens and forms an emulsion.

Heat 1 tablespoon of olive oil in a pan, add the
onion, garlic, saffron, fennel and fennel seeds and
cook for 4–5 minutes until tender. Add the lentils,
paprika and stock and bring to the boil. Cook rapidly
for 2–3 minutes, then reduce the heat and simmer
for 30 minutes. Stir in the spinach leaves and allow
to wilt in the soup.

Toast the bread cubes and place in 4 serving bowls.
Pour over the soup and drizzle over 1 tablespoon of
olive oil. Serve the hot rouille separately.

One of my favourite ways to enjoy smoked fish, this soup has a wonderful rich creamy yet earthy flavour, and is a real meal in itself. Take care to use natural smoked haddock and not the horrible yellow dyed variety.

smoked fish chowder

1 tablespoon cornflour
1 litre full fat milk
2 sprigs of fresh parsley
1 sprig of fresh thyme
1 garlic clove, crushed
350g skinless natural smoked haddock fillet
50g unsalted butter
4 shallots, sliced
2 large potatoes, peeled, cubed
2 carrots, peeled, cubed
1 stick of celery, peeled, sliced
200ml dry white wine
150ml double cream
125g sliced smoked salmon, cut into small pieces
50g sweetcorn kernels
freshly chopped parsley to serve
salt and freshly ground pepper

Mix the cornflour and 4 tablespoons milk to a smooth paste in a bowl. Transfer to a pan along with the herbs and garlic and bring to the boil. Reduce to a simmer for 5 minutes.

Add the smoked haddock and poach for 3–4 minutes until lightly cooked. Remove and flake into pieces. Leave to cool. Strain the milk and leave to one side.

Melt the butter in a pan, add the vegetables and cook for 2–3 minutes, then pour over the wine.

Reduce by half in volume, and then add the cooking milk and cream. Simmer for 10–15 minutes until the vegetables are just cooked and the liquid reduced in consistency.

Stir in the flaked haddock, then add the smoked salmon, sweetcorn and chopped parsley. Season to taste and serve.

A rich, comforting soup from Lancashire – not Scotland, as the name might suggest.

tattie hushie

potato, cauliflower & oatmeal soup

25g unsalted butter
1 leek, sliced
200g cauliflower, cut into small florets
550g floury potatoes, peeled and diced
600ml full fat milk
50g coarse oatmeal
600ml chicken stock
salt and freshly ground black pepper

Heat the butter in a pan, add the leek and cauliflower and cook gently for a few minutes. Add the potatoes, then cover and sweat for 10 minutes. Mix together the milk and oatmeal and pour them over the vegetables.

Add the stock, bring to the boil and simmer until the vegetables are tender. Blitz the soup to a purée in a blender, then reheat gently and season to taste.

PG TIPS
Although my version of this soup is made with cauliflower, the earliest recipes on file originally used leeks instead and the dish was finished off with a little tomato ketchup. I prefer this version.

I love this rustic soup – served with chunks of warm bread it makes a happy meal. Any spicy sausage such as *chorizo* or *merguez* can be substituted for the Polish *kielbasa*.

polish sausage & butter bean soup

1 tablespoon olive oil
225g *kielbasa* sausage, cut into thin
  slices
2 carrots, peeled, chopped
2 sticks celery, peeled, sliced
1 onion, peeled, chopped
pinch of chilli powder
600ml light chicken or vegetable stock
400g tinned tomatoes, chopped
300g Savoy cabbage, shredded
400g tinned butter beans
salt and freshly ground pepper
small bunch of dill
50ml sour cream to serve

Heat the olive oil in a heavy based pan, add the sausage pieces and fry until golden on both sides. Add the carrots, celery, onion and pinch of chilli and cook for 5 minutes.

Add the stock, tomatoes, cabbage and butter beans, then mix and season well. Bring to the boil, then reduce the heat to a simmer. Cook for 10–15 minutes until the vegetables are just tender.

Add the dill and serve. Pass the sour cream separately for diners to add at the table.

A soup that can really satisfy on a chilly winter's night, I've been preparing this family favourite for many years.

honey-roasted parsnip soup

25g unsalted butter
500g parsnips, roughly chopped
½ onion, roughly chopped
1 carrot, roughly chopped
1 small clove garlic, roughly chopped
1 teaspoon thyme leaves
1 small bay leaf
1 tablespoon clear honey
1 litre chicken or vegetable stock
6 tablespoons dry cider
4 tablespoons double cream

Preheat the oven to 220º/425ºF/gas mark 7. Heat the butter in an ovenproof casserole dish, add the parsnips and roast in the oven for 25–30 minutes until golden brown. Add the onion, carrot and garlic and continue cooking for a further 10 minutes, then mix in the herbs and honey. Cook for about 10 minutes more, until the vegetables have caramelised.

Remove the dish from the oven, add the stock and bring to the boil on top of the stove. Reduce the heat and simmer for 10 minutes. Add the cider then pour the soup into a blender and purée until smooth. Strain through a fine strainer, bring back to the boil, remove from the heat, swirl in the cream and serve.

PG TIPS
This soup can be garnished with some diced bread croûtons, fried in butter until golden. Try it prepared in the same way with celeriac or salsify.

chilled soups

A real treat for a hot summer's day, this chilled beetroot
soup is delicately lifted with a little horseradish; try it as it
will soon become a summer favourite.

beetroot gazpacho

with avocado cream

for the frozen avocado cream
150g sugar
65ml water
2 avocados (preferably Haas variety)
250ml dry white wine
juice of ½ lemon
4 tablespoons whipping cream

1kg ripe plum tomatoes, cut into
   small chunks
1 small onion, chopped
1 small green pepper, deseeded, cut
   into small chunks
1 garlic clove, crushed
1 slice of stale bread
5 tablespoons extra virgin olive oil
3 tablespoons good quality sherry
   vinegar
1 tablespoon creamed horseradish
2 roasted beetroot, peeled and
   chopped
1 Granny Smith apple
salt and freshly ground black pepper

For the avocado cream, bring the sugar and water to
the boil and simmer for 1 minute, then cool. Peel the
avocados and cut the flesh into pieces. Blend in a food
processor with the sugar syrup, white wine and lemon
juice. Add the cream, transfer to an ice-cream machine,
churn and freeze overnight.

Place the tomatoes, onion, pepper, garlic and bread in
a food processor and blend to a fine purée. With the
motor running, gently pour in a thin stream of the oil
through the funnel and blend until it thickens and
forms an emulsion. Add the vinegar, horseradish and
beetroot, then blend again until smooth; season to taste.
The flavour should be slightly sweet and sour – add a
little more vinegar if necessary. Chill for 4 hours.

Pour the chilled soup into 4 shallow soup bowls. Peel the
apple, then shred into fine strips using a sharp knife or a
kitchen mandolin. Place a ball of avocado cream in the
centre of each soup and top with shredded apple.

When you feel like splashing out on a special night, this dish could be the one. Although the base of it is made from potatoes and watercress, it is indulgently topped with a good dollop of caviar. Go on, spoil yourself – you deserve it!

chilled potato & watercress soup

2 bunches of watercress
50g unsalted butter
1 onion, chopped
2 leeks, white part only, chopped
450g floury potatoes, peeled and
   diced
900ml chicken stock
120ml double cream
salt and freshly ground black
   pepper

for the caviar chantilly:
100ml double cream, semi-
   whipped
20g caviar or suitable alternative
   (see PG TIPS)

Pick the leaves from one bunch of watercress and set aside. Blanch the other bunch and the stalks in boiling water, then drain, refresh in cold water and drain again. Chop finely.

Heat the butter in a pan, add the onion, leeks and potatoes, then cover and sweat over a low heat until softened. Pour in the chicken stock, add the chopped watercress and bring to the boil. Simmer for 20–25 minutes, until the potatoes are falling apart. Pour the soup into a blender and blitz to a purée. Leave to cool, then stir in the double cream. Season to taste and chill thoroughly.

Pour into serving bowls, garnish with the reserved watercress leaves, then place a dollop of cream in the centre of each portion and top it with the caviar.

PG TIPS
Although nothing can replace the impact of real salty tasting caviar, there are some cheaper farmed varieties and even vegetarian products now available for use.

Intense yet delicate in flavour, this version of vichyssoise makes an ideal soup for early autumn. It's thickened with cream and served chilled, garnished with chives.

pear, celeriac & stilton vichyssoise

25g unsalted butter
1 onion finely diced
300g celeriac, peeled and finely diced
2 ripe pears, peeled, cored and finely diced
1 litre chicken or vegetable stock
750ml single cream
75g Stilton, crumbled
2 tablespoons chopped fresh chives
salt and freshly ground black pepper

Heat the butter in a pan, add the onion and celeriac and cook over a gentle heat until they begin to soften, about 8–10 minutes. Stir in the pears and cook for 3–4 minutes. Add the stock and bring to the boil, then reduce the heat and simmer for 25 minutes, until the vegetables are tender. Remove from the heat, stir in the cream and Stilton and then purée the soup in a blender until smooth. Leave to cool, then chill slightly.

Before serving it may be necessary to thin down the soup with a little milk, stock or cream. Stir in the chives and season to taste.

PG TIPS
I'm often asked what is the correct consistency for puréed soups. In my experience, a good general rule is that they should be approximately the consistency of single cream, thick enough to coat the back of a spoon.

In this welcoming summer soup the fruits take on more definition and texture than in a traditional ceviche, while the drizzle of Thai basil oil adds a magical taste of aniseed.

fruit ceviche soup

with Thai basil oil

for the oil
50g Thai basil (holy basil), available
  from Asian supermarkets
75ml groundnut or vegetable oil

for the soup
200g fresh pineapple, diced
1 ripe mango, diced
1.5cm piece of root ginger, peeled
  and finely grated
1 tablespoon tamarind paste
2 tablespoons maple syrup
300ml fresh orange juice
freshly cracked black pepper

for the fruit ceviche
75g fresh pineapple, cut into 5mm
  dice
½ mango, cut into 5mm dice
small wedge of orange
fresh melon (charentais or
  cantaloupe) cut into 5mm dice
1 small red onion, finely chopped
2 kiwis, cut into 5mm dice
1 pasilla chilli, deseeded, finely
  chopped
juice of 2 limes, zest of 1

For the oil, place the Thai basil and oil in a blender and blitz to a purée, then strain, cover and refrigerate.

For the soup, place the pineapple, mango and ginger in a bowl and leave to marinate at room temperature for 1 hour.

Meanwhile for the ceviche, place all the ingredients in a bowl and toss well together. Set aside.

Place the marinated fruits and ginger in a food processor and add the tamarind paste, maple syrup and orange juice. Blend to a fine purée and then strain or sieve into a bowl. Chill for a good 2–3 hours.

Place the ceviche into the centre of 4 well chilled shallow soup bowls, pour over the soup, crack over some fresh black pepper and drizzle the Thai basil oil over. Serve immediately.

chilled smoky tomato soup

with soured cream

1.5kg ripe but firm plum tomatoes, halved
4 tablespoons olive oil
1 onion, chopped
2 garlic cloves, crushed
2 teaspoons ground cumin
½ teaspoon ground coriander
2 teaspoons smoked paprika, plus extra to garnish
2 Hungarian cherry chilli peppers, deseeded and chopped
1 tablespoon tomato purée
900ml chicken stock
4 tablespoons balsamic vinegar
1½ tablespoons castor sugar
4 tablespoons soured cream
salt and freshly ground black pepper

Preheat the grill to its highest setting. Put the tomatoes in a bowl and toss them with half the olive oil, then place on the grill rack. Place under the hot grill for 8–10 minutes or until they are soft and slightly charred.

Heat the remaining oil in a large pan, add the onion, garlic, cumin, coriander and half the paprika and fry gently until softened but not coloured. Add the chilli peppers, tomatoes and the tomato purée and cook over a low heat for 5 minutes. Pour on the chicken stock and bring to the boil, then reduce the heat and simmer for 2 minutes. Pass the soup through a fine sieve. Add the vinegar and sugar, return the soup to the boil and simmer for 3–5 minutes. Remove from the heat, leave to cool and chill. Season with salt and pepper when cold.

To serve, ladle into individual soup bowls. Blend together the soured cream and the remaining paprika, top each bowlful with a dollop of cream and sprinkle over a little extra paprika. Stir in gently to create a decorative swirl.

PG TIPS
Don't purée this soup in a blender – it tends to lose its colour and becomes a washed out shade of pink.

A wonderful chilled summer soup with flavours redolent of the eastern Mediterranean. *Hummus* means chickpea in Arabic and is made by creating a paste with chickpeas and *tahini*.

chilled hummus, saffron & yogurt soup

1 teaspoon olive oil
1 onion, chopped
2 garlic cloves, crushed
1 teaspoon ground cumin
pinch of saffron
310g dried chickpeas, soaked
    overnight
750ml vegetable stock
1 tablespoon *tahini* (sesame seed
    paste)
100ml low-fat natural yogurt
juice of 1 lemon
2 tablespoons chopped coriander
    leaves
freshly ground black pepper
pinch of paprika

Heat the oil in a pan, add the onion, garlic, cumin and 2 tablespoons water, then cover with a lid. Reduce the heat and cook for 5 minutes. Remove the lid, add the saffron and cook for 2 more minutes. Add the drained chickpeas, cover with the vegetable stock and return to the boil, then reduce the heat and cook for 40–45 minutes until the chickpeas are tender.

Pour the soup into a blender, add the *tahini* and blitz to a smooth paste.

Place in 4 bowls and chill thoroughly. Add the yogurt, lemon juice and chopped coriander and stir. Season with black pepper to taste and serve chilled, sprinkled with paprika.

Another great summer soup, this makes a regular appearance on my menus. It is light and delicately spiced and really gets the gastric juices going. If you are serving the *naan* bread, I recommend it served hot – it makes a good contrast.

cool
cucumber soup

with Indian spices & mint

for the curry paste
2 tablespoons mild curry powder
1 tablespoon *garam masala*
½ teaspoon mustard seeds
1 teaspoon cumin seeds
1 garlic clove, crushed

for the cucumber soup
2 cucumbers, peeled and halved
  lengthways
1 small red chilli, halved, seeds
  removed and finely chopped
700ml thick natural yogurt
2 tablespoons chopped fresh
  mint leaves
little lemon juice
salt and freshly ground black
  pepper

hot *naan* bread, cut into fingers
  (optional)

For the curry paste, put the curry powder and *garam masala* in a bowl. Add 3 tablespoons of water and mix to a paste.

Heat a frying pan over a moderate heat, throw in the mustard and cumin seeds and dry-fry them for 20–30 seconds until they give off an aromatic fragrance. Add 2 teaspoons of the curry paste and garlic, reduce the heat to very low and cook for 1 minute. Remove and leave to cool.

For the cucumber soup, remove the seeds from the cucumbers and cut them into chunks. Place them in a food processor, add the chilli and curry paste and blend to a fairly smooth liquid. Strain through a sieve. Pour into a bowl, whisk in the yogurt, add the mint and a squeeze of lemon juice to taste; season. Refrigerate until needed. Serve in 4 soup bowls with the *naan* bread, if using.

If you have never tasted a chilled avocado soup, you have missed out. For me it's the nicest way to enjoy this buttery tasting fruit.

chilled avocado & ginger soup

2 large, ripe avocados, stoned and peeled
1 garlic clove, chopped
1 onion, chopped
1 green chilli, finely chopped
juice of 2 lemons
750ml vegetable or chicken stock, chilled
½ teaspoon coriander seeds
juice from a 5cm piece of fresh root ginger (see PG TIPS)
2 tablespoons soured cream
4 tablespoons olive oil
salt and freshly ground black pepper

Place the avocado flesh in a blender with the garlic, onion, chilli, lemon juice and stock and blitz to a smooth purée.

In a small hot frying pan, dry toast the coriander seeds for 20 seconds. Add them to the blender with half the ginger juice and blitz again to give a smooth, silky consistency. Transfer the soup to a bowl and whisk in the soured cream. Season with salt and pepper to taste and chill well.

To serve, pour into chilled soup bowls, mix the remaining ginger juice with the olive oil and drizzle it over the soup.

PG TIPS

To obtain natural ginger juice, I grate the ginger and squeeze it through muslin. When grating you will find that the tougher fibres get caught in the grater; these should be discarded.

To add a touch of dinner party elegance, top the soup with some small prawns before serving.

This is a chilled variation of chowder made with buttermilk.
Wild garlic grows wild in plentiful supply in the spring.

buttermilk sweetcorn bisque

with radish & wild garlic

20g unsalted butter
1 onion, chopped
1 stick of celery, chopped
2 garlic cloves, crushed
sprig of fresh thyme
3 corn on the cob, kernels detached,
   cob centres reserved
300ml single cream
100ml buttermilk
salt, freshly ground black pepper and
   a pinch of Cayenne pepper
4 small red radishes
1 small bunch of wild garlic leaves
   (or chives)

Melt the butter in a large pan, add the onion, celery, garlic and thyme and leave to cook over a low heat for 10–12 minutes until the vegetables are soft. Add 750ml water to the vegetables with the cob centres. Bring to the boil, reduce the heat and simmer for 20 minutes over a gentle heat until the liquid becomes flavourful. Remove the cob centres and discard. Add the sweetcorn kernels and cream to the liquid and simmer for 10 minutes. Remove half of the kernels for garnishing and leave to cool.

Transfer the cooled soup to a food processor and blend until smooth. Strain it and then refrigerate until needed.

To serve, add the buttermilk, season with salt, pepper and a pinch of Cayenne and add the reserved kernels to the soup. Pour into 4 individual soup bowls. Garnish with a little pile of grated or shredded red radish and some shredded wild garlic leaves. Serve well chilled.

exotic soups

This is an adaptation of a soup I had in one of America's best-loved Mexican restaurants.

arepa soup

1kg mussels
500g clams
2 shallots, finely sliced
2 green chillies, finely sliced
100ml dry white wine
1 litre chicken stock
150ml full fat milk
100g polenta
200g cooked sweetcorn
100ml double cream
100g small Norwegian prawns
salt and freshly ground black pepper

Scrub the mussels and clams under cold running water, de-bearding the mussels and discarding any open ones that don't close when tapped on a work surface. Place in a large pan with the shallots and half the chillies, pour over the white wine and chicken stock, then cover and cook over a high heat for 3–4 minutes, shaking the pan occasionally, until the shells open. Drain the mussels and clams in a colander, then strain the cooking liquor into a clean pan. Bring to the boil, and add the milk. Rain in the polenta and cook over a low heat, stirring constantly, for 4–5 minutes or until thickened.

Remove the mussels and clams from their shells, reserving a few whole clams to use as a garnish. Place the polenta soup in a blender, add half the mussels and clams and half the sweetcorn and blitz to a smooth purée.

Return to the pan, add the cream and bring to the boil. Season to taste, then add the remaining mussels, clams and sweetcorn, together with the prawns. Serve garnished with whole clams and the remaining chilli.

This soup originates from the South-east Asian country of Thailand. Classic *tom yum* soup contains fish or meat, but this variation using wild mushrooms is equally flavoursome. The use of shiitake mushrooms adds a meaty flavour to the broth.

mushroom tom yum

900ml good vegetable stock
4cm piece of galangal, peeled, cut into thin slices (see PG TIPS, page 77)
2 sticks of lemongrass, outer casing discarded, thinly shredded
1 tablespoon *nam pla* (Thai fish sauce) or vegetarian fish sauce (*nuoc mam chay*)
3 kaffir lime leaves, torn into small pieces
275g wild mushrooms of your choice (including shiitake)
2 teaspoons red Thai curry paste
2 large shallots, thinly sliced
3 tomatoes, cut into 1cm dice
juice of 2 limes
little coarse sea salt
40g fresh coriander leaves

Bring the vegetable stock to the boil, add the galangal and lemongrass and cook for 3–4 minutes. Add the fish sauce, lime leaves and mushrooms and simmer for 5 minutes.

Stir in the curry paste. Add the shallots and diced tomatoes and cook for a further 2 minutes. Finish with the lime juice and a little salt. Taste the soup – it should be spicy, sour and a little salty. Pour into 4 individual soup bowls and scatter over the coriander leaves.

PG TIPS

Although the flavour of fresh lemongrass is superior, it can also be purchased in dried and powdered form, but lacks the zesty citrus flavour of the fresh variety.

A soup with the typical Middle Eastern flavours of fragrant spices and fresh mint, this dish is great for all seasons – perfect as a light meal in the summer or a warming, aromatic starter in winter. Choose herbs that are as fresh as possible to maximise flavour.

persian minted onion soup

1 tablespoon groundnut or
  vegetable oil
4 large onions, thinly sliced
1 teaspoon castor sugar
¼ teaspoon ground turmeric
⅛ teaspoon ground cinnamon
⅛ teaspoon ground cardamom
2 tablespoons flour
1 litre chicken stock
3 tablespoons lemon juice
3 tablespoons lime juice
2 tablespoons chopped mint leaves

Heat the oil in a heavy based pan. Add the onions, sugar, turmeric, cinnamon and cardamom and 4 tablespoons water, cover with a lid and cook over a moderate heat for 10–15 minutes, stirring regularly until all the liquid has evaporated, leaving the onions tender, caramelised and golden.

Sprinkle over the flour and cook over a reduced heat for 2 minutes. Gradually add the chicken stock, stirring regularly, and then bring to the boil. Reduce the heat and simmer for 40 minutes.

Mix together the lemon and lime juices, then add to the soup and simmer for a further 10 minutes.

Stir in the mint, and serve immediately.

A really satisfying noodle soup from Indonesia and Malaysia. There are many recipes for *laksa*, using chicken, fish or prawns, but this one is ideal for vegetarians. The list of ingredients may look long but it is simple to prepare.

sweet potato laksa

3 tablespoons groundnut or
　vegetable oil
200g pressed beancurd, cut into 1cm
　cubes
1 onion, finely chopped
2 garlic cloves, crushed
350g orange-fleshed sweet potatoes,
　peeled and cut into 1cm cubes
25g macadamia nuts, ground
1 teaspoon ground cumin
1 teaspoon ground coriander
2 small red chillies, deseeded and
　thinly sliced
½ teaspoon *blachan* (shrimp paste)
1½ tablespoons yellow (or red) Thai
　curry paste
300ml vegetable or chicken stock
600ml coconut milk
1 tablespoon brown sugar
zest of 1 lime, finely grated
250g flat rice noodles
200g beansprouts
4 spring onions, shredded
1 tablespoon chopped coriander
1 tablespoon chopped mint
salt and freshly ground black pepper

Heat 1 tablespoon of the oil in a large pan, add the beancurd and fry until golden and crisp. Remove from the pan and set aside.

Heat the remaining oil in the pan, add the onion and garlic and cook over a medium heat until softened. Add the sweet potatoes and toss with the onion and garlic. Stir in the ground macadamia nuts, cumin, coriander, half the chilli and the *blachan* and cook for 2 minutes. Add the curry paste and cook for 5 minutes to release the fragrance. Stir in the stock and bring to the boil, then add the coconut milk, sugar and lime zest. Reduce the heat to a simmer and cook for a further 10 minutes.

Cook the rice noodles in boiling water for 5 minutes and then drain. Place them in 4 deep soup bowls and top with the fried beancurd. Stir the beansprouts into the soup, season to taste, and pour over the noodles. Sprinkle the spring onions, coriander, mint and remaining chilli on top, and serve.

asparagus consommé

with lemongrass

400g asparagus
25g unsalted butter
1 small onion, thinly sliced
1 small leek, white part only, sliced
2 lemongrass stalks, roughly chopped
900ml chicken stock
3 free-range egg whites
salt and freshly ground black pepper

Peel the asparagus and keep the peelings. Cut off about 5cm of each asparagus tip and set aside. Roughly chop the stalks. Heat the butter in a pan, add the onion and leek and cook over a low heat for 5–8 minutes, until tender. Add the asparagus peelings and stalks and the lemongrass and sweat for 5 minutes. Pour in the stock, bring to the boil, then reduce the heat and simmer for about 30–40 minutes.

Cook the asparagus tips in a pan of boiling water for 5 minutes, then drain, refresh under cold water and drain again. Cut into thin slices on the diagonal and set aside.

Strain the stock through a fine sieve and leave to cool. To clarify it, lightly beat the egg whites just to break them up and then mix them into the stock. Pour into a large pan, bring gently to the boil and watch until the stock begins to bubble through the egg white crust that forms. Reduce the heat and simmer for about 10 minutes, until the soup begins to clear. Place a large sieve lined with muslin or a thin tea towel over a large bowl. Make a hole in the egg white crust and ladle the clear consommé through the sieve.

Reheat and season to taste. Garnish with the asparagus tips and serve immediately.

If you can find Thai basil, which is sometimes available from Asian grocer's shops, the soup will have a more authentic flavour. But it's delicious made with ordinary basil, too.

thai-inspired pumpkin & basil soup

25g unsalted butter
450g pumpkin or butternut squash, peeled and cut into 1cm dice
1 onion, chopped
2 garlic cloves, crushed
1 teaspoon finely chopped fresh galangal or ginger
1 Thai chilli, thinly sliced
1 tablespoon red Thai curry paste
1 litre chicken stock
175ml coconut milk
8 basil leaves, torn into small pieces
salt and freshly ground black pepper

Heat the butter in a frying pan, add the diced pumpkin and fry for 3–4 minutes, until coloured. Add the onion, garlic, galangal or ginger, and chilli and cook for 2 minutes. Stir in the paste and cook for 1 minute, until fragrant. Add the chicken stock and bring to the boil, then reduce the heat and simmer until the pumpkin is just tender.

Finally, stir in the coconut milk and torn basil leaves and season to taste. Serve in 4 individual bowls.

PG TIPS

Galangal is often called blue ginger, but although it resembles ginger, there is little further similarity. Galangal has a unique camphorised flavour, and is available from Asian grocers and markets.

An oriental-inspired light soup, both delicate and interesting in flavour. Here I use clams, a favourite ingredient of mine, but you could substitute mussels or mixed seafood if preferred. Supermarkets now sell packets of cooked, mixed seafood for convenience.

hot & sour clam broth

1 teaspoon sugar
1 tablespoon lime juice
1 tablespoon soy sauce
750ml chicken stock
1 garlic clove, crushed
4 spring onions, finely shredded
75g shiitake mushrooms, sliced
75g *pak choi*, finely shredded
2.5cm piece of fresh root ginger,
   thinly shredded
500g baby clams
½ teaspoon chilli oil
freshly ground black pepper

Mix together the sugar, lime juice and soy sauce.

In a pan, bring the stock to the boil, add the garlic, vegetables and ginger and simmer for 8–10 minutes. Add the clams and cook for a further 2 minutes until they open. Add the sugar and juice mixture and cook for a further minute.

Remove from the heat, add the chilli oil, season to taste with black pepper and serve in deep bowls.

PG TIPS

Shiitake mushrooms have a very meaty flavour that has grown in popularity the world over. They are available fresh, or dried. Originally native to East Asia, Holland and Russia both now cultivate and export vast amounts of this tasty fungus.

Using the classic bisque of France as a base, I added a little tamarind to give it a slight sharpness that really works well. If using frozen tiger prawns, ensure that they are fully defrosted before use. A great soup for a dinner party.

prawn tamarind soup

1 tablespoon olive oil
500g fresh or frozen tiger prawns, shelled and deveined
1 onion, chopped
1 garlic clove, crushed
1 small red chilli, deseeded and chopped
1 tablespoon tomato purée
1 tablespoon plain flour
4 tomatoes, chopped
1 tablespoon tamarind paste
2 lemongrass sticks, finely chopped
1 litre fish stock (or water)
1 teaspoon *nam pla* (fish sauce)
juice of ½ lime
1 tablespoon palm sugar (or demerara)
pinch of Cayenne pepper

Heat the oil in a heavy based pan. When hot, add the prawn shells and fry until red, stirring them constantly. Remove and set aside. Add the onion, garlic and chilli to the pan and fry for 2–3 minutes. Stir in the tomato purée and mix well.

Sprinkle over the flour, mix well and cook for a further 2 minutes. Add the tomatoes, tamarind paste, lemongrass and stock and bring to the boil, then reduce the heat and simmer for 30–35 minutes.

Strain through a fine sieve into a clean pan and add the *nam pla*, lime juice, palm sugar and Cayenne. Chop the prawns roughly into bite-sized pieces and cook in the soup for 1 minute before serving.

PG TIPS
If palm sugar is not available, simply replace with brown sugar in the recipe.

A hot and colourful soup from India, whose name translates as 'black pepper water'. It is highly peppery, with a base of lentils and tamarind.

rasam

1 onion, finely chopped
2 garlic cloves, chopped
2.5cm piece of fresh galangal or
  ginger, finely chopped
1 heaped teaspoon black
  peppercorns
¼ teaspoon cumin seeds
¼ teaspoon coriander seeds
1 litre chicken stock
125g yellow lentils
2 plum tomatoes, peeled,
  deseeded and chopped
50g sweetcorn kernels
4 spring onions, shredded
1 red chilli, deseeded and thinly
  sliced
1 teaspoon tamarind paste
1 teaspoon brown sugar
2 tablespoons chopped coriander
salt

Crush the onion, garlic, galangal or ginger, black peppercorns, cumin and coriander seeds with a pestle and mortar. Place in a saucepan, pour in the stock and bring to the boil.

Reduce the heat, add the lentils and simmer gently for 40–45 minutes, until the lentils are tender. Add the vegetables, red chilli, tamarind paste and sugar and cook for a further 5 minutes.

Season with a little salt, add the chopped coriander and serve.

PG TIPS

I always advise buying spices such as cumin and coriander in the smallest amounts possible. Once opened, they will lose their potency and strength over a short period. In any event, keep them in an airtight container until needed.

Japanese artichokes, or crosnes, are hard to find except from specialist greengrocers. If you cannot obtain them, simply replace with Jerusalem artichokes.

japanese artichoke & rocket soup

700g Japanese artichokes, trimmed
salt and freshly ground black pepper
25g unsalted butter
1 onion, finely chopped
750ml vegetable stock
150ml milk
a good handful of rocket leaves, shredded
freshly grated nutmeg

Unless the Japanese artichokes are very young, blanch them in a large pan of boiling water for 10–15 seconds, drain well, then put them in a tea towel with a little coarse salt and rub gently to remove the skins.

Heat the butter in a large saucepan, add the onion, then cover and sweat for 10 minutes, until soft. Add the artichokes and sweat for 5 minutes. Remove a cupful of the artichokes, cut any large ones in half and set aside.

Add the stock and milk to the artichokes in the pan and bring to the boil. Reduce the heat and simmer for 20 minutes or until the artichokes are tender. Add the shredded rocket leaves and season with salt, pepper and nutmeg. Transfer to a blender and blitz to a light purée. Reheat the soup and check the seasoning. Stir in the reserved artichokes and serve immediately.

Chermoula is the name given to a blend of herbs, spices, oil and lemon juice normally used as a marinade for fish or meat. In my variation it is more of a sauce. It will make far more than you need but you can use it in all manner of ways – as a salad dressing, for pasta or as a vibrant, zesty side sauce. *Chermoula* will keep in the fridge for 3–4 days but will lose its bright colour after 2 days.

moroccan carrot soup

with *chermoula*

25g unsalted butter
1cm piece of fresh ginger, very finely chopped
¼ teaspoon ground turmeric
¼ teaspoon ground cumin
1 onion, chopped
1 leek, white part only, chopped
450g carrots, cut into small chunks
¼ teaspoon paprika
1 litre vegetable stock
salt and freshly ground black pepper

for the *chermoula*
120g fresh coriander
1 garlic clove, crushed
¼ teaspoon ground coriander
¼ teaspoon ground cumin
100ml olive oil
juice of ¼ lemon

Heat the butter in a large pan, add the ginger, turmeric and cumin and sweat for 1–2 minutes. Add the onion, leek and carrots and sweat for 5 minutes. Stir in the paprika and then pour in the vegetable stock. Bring to the boil, then reduce the heat and simmer until the vegetables are tender, about 30 minutes. Purée in a blender until smooth, then reheat and season to taste.

For the *chermoula*, put all the ingredients in a blender and blitz to a smooth paste. Serve the soup in individual bowls, spooning about a tablespoon of *chermoula* over each portion.

PG TIPS
Chermoula is also delicious blended into a well-flavoured mayonnaise, then spread on thick slices of bread and used to make a chicken, prawn or tuna sandwich – sheer heaven!

lemongrass & crab broth

750ml fish or chicken stock
400g can of chopped tomatoes
2 teaspoons grated fresh root ginger
  (or galangal)
4 lemongrass stalks, white part only,
  halved lengthways
2 kaffir lime leaves
100g Chinese vermicelli rice noodles
1 teaspoon brown sugar
1 garlic clove, crushed
1½ teaspoons *nam pla* (Thai fish
  sauce)
450g fresh white crabmeat
4 spring onions, finely shredded
handful of baby spinach leaves
  (optional)
salt and freshly ground black pepper
8 Thai basil leaves, torn into small
  pieces

Put the stock in a saucepan with the tomatoes,
ginger, lemongrass and kaffir lime leaves and bring
to the boil. Reduce the heat and simmer for 8–10
minutes, then remove and discard the lemongrass.
Add the noodles, sugar and garlic and simmer for
3–4 minutes.

Stir in the fish sauce, crabmeat, spring onions and
spinach, if using, and heat through for 2 minutes.
Season to taste, sprinkle over the Thai basil and
serve immediately.

PG TIPS

Thai basil has a lovely enticing fragrance, a subtle
flavour of liquorice and aniseed. It is the herb that
gives Thai curries their wonderful taste and aroma.
It is also fantastic added to Asian salads, made of
meat or fish. To store, wrap in damp kitchen paper
or a damp J-cloth and keep in the fridge.

show stoppers

roasted sweet potato bisque

with avocado & lime salsa

650g sweet potatoes, peeled and cut
   into large chunks
6 tablespoons olive oil
1 onion, finely chopped
1 garlic clove, crushed
5cm piece of fresh root ginger, grated
1 small red chilli, deseeded and
   thinly sliced
½ teaspoon ground cinnamon
salt and freshly ground black pepper
750ml vegetable or chicken stock
120ml double cream
2 tablespoons maple syrup
juice of 2 limes

for the salsa
1 avocado, peeled, stoned and cut
   into small cubes
2 plum tomatoes, skinned, deseeded
   and chopped
4 tablespoons lime juice
2 spring onions, chopped
1 small red chilli, deseeded and
   chopped
1 tablespoon roughly chopped
   coriander
3 tablespoons olive oil

Preheat the oven to 200°C/400°F/gas mark 6.
Place the sweet potatoes in a baking tin, pour over
4 tablespoons of the olive oil and roast for 40 minutes
or until tender – don't let them brown too much.

Heat the remaining oil in a large pan, add the
onion, garlic and grated ginger and cook gently for
5 minutes. Add the roasted sweet potatoes, red chilli,
cinnamon and some seasoning, then pour in the
stock and bring to the boil. Reduce the heat and
simmer for 15 minutes. Pour the soup into a blender
and blitz to a smooth purée, then pour it into a large
bowl. Stir in the double cream, maple syrup and lime
juice and chill thoroughly.

For the salsa, put the avocado cubes in a bowl, add
all the remaining ingredients and mix well. Season
to taste.

To serve, pour the soup into chilled soup bowls and
place a spoonful of avocado and lime salsa in the
centre of each one.

roasted pepper passata

with basil yogurt

for the passata
8 ripe plum tomatoes, halved
2 red peppers, halved, deseeded
  and chopped small
1 onion, quartered
2 garlic cloves, peeled
sprig of fresh thyme
2 tablespoons olive oil
salt and freshly ground black
  pepper
900ml good vegetable stock, hot
1 tablespoon tomato purée

for the basil yogurt
50g fresh basil leaves
40ml extra virgin olive oil
4 tablespoons natural thick set
  yogurt

for the tomato tartare
2 plum tomatoes, blanched and
  seeded
1 small garlic clove, crushed
1 tablespoon maple syrup
juice of ½ lime
1 tablespoon chopped fresh basil

Preheat the oven to 220°C/425°F/gas mark 7. Place the tomatoes, peppers, onion, garlic and thyme in a roasting tin, spoon over the olive oil and season. Roast them for 20–25 minutes, until wilted and slightly charred all over (alternatively, this could be done under a hot grill). Transfer to a pan, pour over the stock and add the tomato purée. Cook over a moderate heat for 15 minutes. Strain the soup through a sieve or strainer and return it to a clean pan, adjust the seasoning and keep warm.

For the yogurt, blanch the basil leaves for 15 seconds in boiling water, then remove immediately with a slotted spoon into iced water. Dry the blanched leaves in a cloth. Place the leaves in a small blender with the olive oil and blitz until smooth. Break down the yogurt with a small whisk to a creamy texture and stir in the basil oil.

For the tomato tartare, mix all the ingredients in a bowl and season to taste. Reheat the soup to boiling point, then pour into 4 bowls. Place 2 good spoonfuls of yogurt in the centre of each bowl, followed by a good spoonful of basil on top. Place a little chilled tomato tartare to one side and serve immediately, accompanied by crisp melba toasts.

A heartwarming, lightly spiced soup topped with stringy fontina cheese and spiked with lemon. Serve with chunks of fresh bread.

cannellini bean soup

with *gremolata*

50 unsalted butter
75g onions, diced
1 garlic clove, crushed
200g cannellini beans, soaked overnight and then drained
50g carrot, diced
½ red chilli, deseeded and finely chopped
2 ripe tomatoes, chopped
2 cardamom pods, crushed
1 teaspoon cumin seeds
1.3 litres chicken or vegetable stock
salt and freshly ground black pepper

for the *gremolata*
75g fontina cheese, (or other strong cheese such as Raclette or Taleggio) very finely grated
1 tablespoon finely grated lemon zest
1 tablespoon fresh thyme leaves
2 garlic cloves, crushed

Melt the butter in a pan over a medium heat, add the onions and garlic and sauté for 4–5 minutes, until softened. Add the cannellini beans, carrot, chilli and tomatoes, then cover and cook gently for 5 minutes. Next, stir in the cardamom, cumin seeds and stock and bring to the boil. Reduce the heat and simmer for 1–1½ hours, or until the beans are tender. Pour the soup into a blender and blitz to a purée, then strain it through a fine sieve to give a creamy texture. Adjust the seasoning and reheat gently.

For the *gremolata*, mix all the ingredients together in a bowl. Pour the soup into warm bowls, scatter with the *gremolata* and serve straight away.

PG TIPS

Other pulses such as lentils can be used equally effectively for this soup. I sometimes leave the beans whole and top them with the *gremolata* to serve as a winter stew.

This soup is typical of many Middle Eastern and North African soups, earthy and rustic. Cardamom is one of my favourite spices but the soup is more likely to be found flavoured with cumin instead.

lebanese lentil soup

4 tablespoons olive oil
1 onion, finely chopped
1 garlic clove, crushed
200g red lentils
1 tablespoon freshly ground
   cardamom
¼ teaspoon ground allspice
½ teaspoon grated lemon zest
1 litre meat stock
salt and freshly ground black pepper
25g unsalted butter
3 slices of white bread, crusts
   removed, cut into 5mm dice
2 tablespoons lemon juice
a few roughly crushed cardamom
   seeds, to garnish

Heat half the oil in a large pan, add the onion and garlic and cook for 2–3 minutes, until softened. Add the lentils and stir until coated in the oil. Add the cardamom, allspice and lemon zest, then pour in the stock and bring to the boil. Reduce the heat and simmer for about 30 minutes, until the lentils are very tender. Cool slightly, then blitz to a coarse textured purée in a blender. Return to the pan, reheat gently and season to taste.

Heat the butter in a large frying pan and fry the diced bread in it until golden. Stir the lemon juice and the remaining oil into the soup, add the bread croûtons, then garnish with the crushed cardamom and serve immediately.

PG TIPS
Replace the lentils with some pre-soaked or canned chickpeas – both would work equally well in this soup. Chickpeas are edible legumes, high in protein and one of the earliest cultivated vegetables on record.

Make this soup when fresh sweetcorn is at the height of its season. The bacon is added at the last minute to retain its crispness, the cheese allowed to melt on top of the soup.

corn bisque

with cheese & smoked bacon

3 corn on the cob
300ml whole milk
25g unsalted butter
1 onion, chopped
1 celery stalk, chopped
25g plain flour
300ml chicken or vegetable
    stock
150g Cheddar cheese, grated
salt and freshly ground black pepper
75g piece of smoked bacon, thinly
    sliced

Remove the husks from the corn, then hold each cob upright on a work surface and cut off the kernels with a knife. Put the kernels in a pan with the milk and bring to the boil. Reduce the heat and simmer for 10–15 minutes, until tender. Drain the corn, reserving the milk.

Melt the butter in a saucepan and gently sauté the onion and celery in it until soft. Add the flour, cook for 2–3 minutes over a low heat and then gradually stir in the milk and stock. Slowly bring to the boil, stirring all the time, until thickened. Reduce the heat and simmer for 15–20 minutes. Add the corn and half the cheese and cook very gently for 5 minutes, then pour into a blender and blitz to a purée. Reheat and season to taste.

Grill the bacon slices until crisp, then crumble them. Sprinkle the bacon over the soup with the remaining cheese just before serving.

PG TIPS
Leeks or spinach would make good alternatives to the sweetcorn.

tomato
gazpacho

with goat's cheese-stuffed tomatoes

for the *gazpacho* soup
900g overripe plum tomatoes (or use
    half plum tomatoes, half beef
    tomatoes)
1 tablespoon tomato ketcup
1 tablespoon olive oil
1 small garlic clove, peeled
1 tablespoon castor sugar
150ml vegetable or chicken stock
bunch fresh basil
2 tablespoons red wine vinegar
2 tablespoons dry vermouth
salt and freshly ground white pepper

for the stuffed tomatoes
2 small firm goat's cheeses (Cabécou
    is my preference)
½ onion, very finely chopped
1 small courgette, very finely
    chopped
1 egg yolk
25g mixed fresh herbs, such as basil,
    chervil, parsley and chives, finely
    chopped
2–3 tablespoons fresh white
    breadcrumbs
8 ripe but firm small tomatoes
a little olive oil for brushing

For the soup, blanch the tomatoes in boiling water for 1 minute, then drain and refresh in ice-cold water. Drain again, then peel, cut in half and put in a bowl with the tomato ketchup, olive oil, garlic, sugar, stock and all but 8–12 leaves from the bunch of basil. Stir in the red wine vinegar and vermouth, season lightly and leave to marinate for 1–2 hours.

Strain the tomato mixture through a fine sieve into a bowl, pushing hard to extract all the juice. Adjust the seasoning, then chill until ready to serve.

For the stuffed tomatoes, preheat the oven to 180°C/350°F/gas mark 4. Put the goat's cheese in a bowl and crush with a fork. Stir in the onion, courgette, egg yolk and herbs, then add enough breadcrumbs to bind the mixture lightly together. Season to taste. Slice the top off each tomato and reserve. Carefully scoop out the pulp and seeds from the tomatoes with a spoon. Fill them with the stuffing, brush with a little olive oil and bake for 5 minutes until soft and heated through.

Place 2 stuffed tomatoes in each soup plate and replace their lids, then carefully pour the *gazpacho* around. Decorate with the reserved basil leaves and serve.

lobster bisque

with cheese

1 cooked lobster, weighing about
  750g
75g unsalted butter
½ onion, roughly chopped
1 celery stick, roughly chopped
1 carrot, roughly chopped
2 garlic cloves, crushed
2 tablespoons tomato purée
4 tablespoons cognac
150ml dry white wine
1 tablespoon fresh tarragon leaves,
  plus a few sprigs to garnish
75g plain flour
1 litre chicken stock
150ml double cream
75g cheese (Lincolnshire Poacher
  is my favourite, or a classic
  Cheddar)
Cayenne pepper
salt and freshly ground pepper

Split the lobster in half down the back: put a large knife through the centre of the body section and cut down through the head, then take out the knife, turn the lobster round and cut down the centre of the body through the tail. Remove and discard the head sac and the intestinal vein, then remove the cooked lobster flesh from the head and tail. Crack the claws in 2 or 3 places and pick out the meat. Place the lobster shells in a bowl and crush them into smallish pieces using a meat hammer to extract maximum flavour.

Heat the butter in a heavy based pan, add the crushed lobster shells and fry for 4–5 minutes, until they begin to turn golden. Add the vegetabes and garlic and fry for 5 minutes, until softened. Stir in the tomato purée, then add the cognac, white wine and tarragon leaves and cook for 5 minutes. Stir in the flour and cook for a further 5 minutes. Add the stock, bring to the boil, and skim off any impurities that rise to the surface. Reduce the heat and simmer for 30–40 minutes.

Meanwhile, dice the lobster flesh and set aside. Bring the cream to the boil in a separate pan, then remove from the heat. Add the cheese and stir until melted and smooth, then set aside.

Blitz the soup in a blender until the shells are quite finely ground, then pass it through a very fine sieve and stir in the cheese cream. Add Cayenne, salt and pepper to taste, then pour into warm bowls. Garnish with the diced lobster and sprigs of tarragon, dust very lightly with Cayenne and serve.

Peas and mint are a classic British combination, and fantastic in this summery soup. When broad beans are in season I often use them to replace the peas. By quickly cooking the vegetables, they retain their colour and natural taste.

english pea & mint soup

with truffle ricotta foam

400g fresh or frozen peas
20g fresh mint leaves
1 onion, chopped
1 leek, chopped
750ml vegetable stock
270ml skimmed milk
1 tablespoon extra virgin olive oil
20g unsalted butter
salt and freshly cracked black pepper
1 teaspoon truffle oil
15g unsalted butter
2 tablespoons ricotta cheese

Bring a large pan of boiling salted water to the boil. Add the peas, mint leaves, onion and leek and simmer gently for about 5–6 minutes until tender. Drain them in a colander, then refresh under cold running water. When they are fully drained, transfer to a food processor and blend to a smooth purée, scraping down the sides once or twice to ensure all the purée is satiny smooth.

Place the vegetable stock and 150ml milk in a pan, add the purée, olive oil and butter and bring to the boil, whisking frequently. Season with salt and freshly cracked black pepper.

In another pan, bring the remaining 120ml milk, truffle oil and butter to the boil. Add the ricotta and blitz with a hand-held blender until smooth and frothy. Divide the soup between 4 bowls, then spoon over the ricotta foam to serve.

In Greece *avgolemeno* is a popular soup made in all manner of ways. I have enjoyed it with chicken and with fish, both equally delicious. I recently enjoyed this recipe on a trip to the beautiful island of Crete. The name *avgolemeno* translated means 'egg and lemon'.

avgolemeno

1 litre chicken stock
75g short grain rice, well washed
3 small eggs
50ml double cream
juice of 2 small lemons
salt and freshly ground white pepper

Bring the chicken stock to the boil in a pan, add the rice and simmer for about 20 minutes or until the rice is tender.

Lightly beat the eggs in a bowl with the double cream and lemon juice. Gradually pour 5–6 tablespoons of the hot rice liquid into the egg mixture, beating all the time.

Return the mixture into the remaining rice soup and remove immediately from the heat, stirring continuously (do not let it curdle).

Season to taste and serve immediately.

PG TIPS

If your lemons are not yielding much juice, put them in the microwave for 20–30 seconds to heat them and their inner juices. Take care when cutting them as the juices get mighty hot!

index